Prepper Hacks Handbook

Survival Hacks, Tips and Tricks

Steve Rayder

Steve Rayder

SOUTHSHORE
PUBLICATIONS & DISTRIBUTION

www.southshorepublications.com

ISBN- 978-1512273502

ISBN-10: 1512273503

Prepper Hacks

CONTENTS

1. INTRODUCTION

As Preppers, we tend to like clever little survival hacks and multiuse items. Partly because we like to use them, and party because we want to show off our clever tricks and tips to our family and friends! So for my latest book I have decided to write a whole book dedicated to them.

There's so many interesting little tips and tricks I have picked up along the way, along with some items that have a whole host of applications that you may never have considered before.

I feel like this information isn't just very useful, but it could also really help you out if you were ever in a SHTF or WROL situation. For those of you who are new to the Prepping game, that means Sh*t Hitting the Fan (referring to the breakdown of society) and Without Rule of Law. So this book is a must read for anyone interested in the survival and preparedness lifestyle.

Firstly I have dedicated a few chapters to certain topics, then the last chapter is the other mini hacks that I couldn't leave out. So, let's get started!

2. BATTERY HACKS

In a SHTF scenario you may be in a situation where you have batteries but they may not be the right size or type of battery you need. Luckily there are a couple of little tricks you can utilize to enable you to use almost any battery for any other use.

If you have a 9 volt battery and you need something like AAA's or AA's then you can actually still use a 9 volt for this purpose. If you get a pair of pliers ideally, or a knife if you're very careful, then you can remove the outer casing of the 9 volt battery. Inside there are 6 cylindrical cells that are just slightly smaller than a AAA battery.

These smaller batteries will fit into the slots for AAA's and AA's but as they are smaller there will be some left over room. All you have to do is bulk out the space with some balls of tin foil. The tin foil will hold the battery in place and, as it is metal and therefore conducts electricity, it will create the electrical connection.

One thing to remember when doing this is that, in the cells that come out of the 9 volt battery, the positive and negative ends are reversed. So the ends with the little circle on them that look like the top of a traditional battery are actually negative and the flat end is positive.

The slightly less common A23 battery also contains a lot of smaller cells inside it, this time they are the flat circular type. So this is another way you can find the right type of battery for your equipment if you needed them.

You can actually use these flat batteries to create a mini light using just one of these batteries and a single LED. LED's have two metal prongs protruding from the bottom. Just slip a flat battery between the prongs and you will have a mini LED light.

Another thing you can do, if you're using a flashlight and you don't have right size batteries, is to actually use the bulb and the wire from the flashlight. Just remove the bulb and some of the wire and connect it up to whatever battery you want. You will have to break the flashlight but if you're desperate then this is a valid option and it's better than nothing at all.

Steve Rayder

3. WATER HACKS

Here's a couple of ways of gathering water when you're desperate. Technique number one is to simply ring out moss. If it has rained recently you can gather a lot of water very quickly by doing this. Another way is to get some fabric such as a shemagh, drag it though dew covered long grass in the morning and then ring it out over a container.

This one is a commonly known one, but some people might be unclear on the exact method. An easy way to clean up muddy, brown water ready for boiling is to make a primitive water filter. To do this simply take some kind of container, like an upturned plastic bottle with the bottom cut off, then stuff some fabric in the end to block up the nozzle, but still allow water to pass through. Next grind up some charcoal from your fire and pour it over the fabric. Then add a layer of sand and finally a layer of grass.

The grass filters out the large debris, the sand filters the medium sized particles and the charcoal takes out the microscopic stuff such as chemicals. Then you can boil this water and it will be as clean as you're going to get without either having professional equipment or distilling it.

If you do drink water that isn't properly filtered and boiled, you could end up with some kind of intestinal problem such as dysentery. To remedy this, simply boil some acorns in some properly filtered water. Acorns are rich in tannic acid, these tannins will turn the water brown and create a kind of medicinal tea that will help stop diarrhea and ease your symptoms.

Bleach is useful for making water safe to drink without the use of fire. This may sound dangerous as obviously drinking bleach generally isn't a great idea, but it's actually not dangerous when it is highly diluted and not done for an extremely extended time period. It will however destroy anything harmful in the water.

To purify water with bleach you need clean the sediment from the water using some kind of water filtration set up. Then once your water is free of sediment, add 4 drops of bleach per liter of warm water and leave it to sit for half an hour. If you can't warm your water in any way then just double the dose but it will taste quite bleachy.

Iodine can also be used in the same way and it's safer for human consumption than bleach. Side note, it is recommended that you don't use Iodine for water purification for longer 6 months straight. For those of you worried about a nuclear disaster, Iodine is also absorbed by your thyroid and will protect it against radiation, bonus!

If you don't like the taste of Iodine you can keep an eye out for some vitamin C tablets on your scavenging missions as they will neutralize the Iodine and make your water taste a lot better.

4. COOKING HACKS

Many cups that are provided with survival gear are solid stainless steel. If you want to drink a hot drink from these cups then you will more often than not, end up burning yourself on the hot metal. A simple trick to avoid this is to add a strip of duct tape to the rim. This will add a layer of insulation between your mouth and the hot metal, protecting you from being burnt.

If you're tired of your mess tins and other types of metal cookware getting charred and stained there's an easy way around this. Just rub some washing up liquid on the outside before you start cooking. This will stop the soot from the fire and the burn marks from the flames from sticking to and staining your cookware.

If you need a grill for cooking while you're out in the woods, try and scavenge a metal rake. Not only are they great for helping you collect leaves for waterproofing a debris shelter, they can also be used as a great makeshift grill.

One problem you are likely to run into if you're out in the woods for an extended period of time is bland food. To add some flavor to your squirrel, try looking for some natural herbs and placing them over the fire with your meat. The smoky herb flavor will make all kinds of meat far more bearable. You can also plan ahead and fill some TicTac boxes with your favorite herbs and spices, these rectangular containers will fit together and take up less space in your bag than normal spice containers.

Now this may surprise you but if you're stuck without a can opener, there's no need to blunt you knife and spend time hacking through the can. All you need to do is find a bit of concrete. If you turn the can upside down and rub it vigorously on the surface of the concrete for a few seconds, the metal lip on the top of the can will wear down allowing you to simply pull the lid straight off.

If you need a platform to raise your mess tins or canteen above the fire, you can just use four tent pegs and build the fire around them. This will give you a stable cooking platform ready for when you need it.

Steve Rayder

5. FIRE HACKS

A fast and easy way to find tinder in wet conditions is to use a pencil sharpener. In wet weather, it may look like all of the wood around you is wet and therefore no good for lighting a fire, but only the outside is actually wet. If you choose wood that isn't lying on the ground it will not have had as much of a chance to soak up the rain water. If you run a thin branch through a pencil sharpener, it will create fine shavings of the dry core of the branch. This makes fantastic tinder in all conditions, but is particularly useful for wet weather.

If you're low on fire starting materials or don't have any good options for igniting a fire. One technique that has been used for longer than I would like to guess at is fire transportation. This great little hack will enable you to move a fire from one place to another without having to relight it and it's easier than you might think.

An easy way of doing this is to use mushrooms. This might sound strange but mushrooms such as Daldinia Concentrica, also called cramp balls and coal fungus, are great for transporting fire. They are easy to identify because they are black and look just like a lump of coal. If you break these mushrooms open, the core will catch a spark from a ferro rod easily and will burn slowly for a very long time. This means they also make great, slow burning tinder. The slow burn will give you plenty of time to get one burning from your existing fire and travel to your new camp where you can then light a new fire using the mushroom as tinder.

A fantastic time saving fire hack is to build an upside down fire. This type of fire will not only feed itself, meaning it will happily burn away and lay down a bed of embers for you without you having to do anything, but it also gives out less smoke than a standard fire and can provide overnight warmth.

To make an upside down fire, all you have to do is stack your large fuel wood on the bottom with the wood getting gradually smaller towards the top. Then on the top add you kindling and tinder bundle. When you light this fire the hot embers will begin to ignite the fire and burn downwards. This means you can go and do other things and carry out other tasks around camp while the fire burns itself down and creates embers that will be ready to cook on when you get back.

If you are using a fire to signal for help then a great tip is to make a flammable torch that you can ignite at a moment's notice to increase you chance of being spotted. To do this quickly and easily, all you need to do is split a branch down the center, go about 10 inches down. Then pack the split with some dry birch bark. Birch bark will ignite very quickly and burn fiercely. If you do need to signal someone then you just have to quickly light it off of your fire and you can run to wherever they have the best chance of seeing you from and wave it about.

Another great tip for signal fires is to place living, green tree boughs over a well-established fire. This will send a plume of thick white smoke up into the sky making your chances of being discovered much higher.

A good way to lower your fires visibility, particularly at night, and to also retain as much heat from your fire as possible is to build a fire reflector wall. You can do this using natural materials, but a much easier and more effective way is to simply use a space blanket. This will block your fire from being seen as easily and giving away your location. It will also reflect back a lot of heat that would have otherwise be lost, enabling you to have a smaller fire and use less wood.

Another largely overlooked use for fires is to fire harden wooden tools. For example, if you have a spear head that you have carved into the end of a branch, simply hold it over the fire just above the flames. This will cause the moisture to evaporate from the wood resulting in a much stronger point.

Steve Rayder

6. EASY NATURAL REMEDIES

I think everyone has probably heard about using Dock leaves to treat stinging nettle stings. This isn't just an old wives tale, it actually does work on a variety of different stings and bites. This is because Dock leaves contain a natural antihistamine. To increase its effectiveness, chew on the leaf for a few seconds to break up the fibers and apply it to the sting.

The inner bark of the willow tree contains salicylic acid. This can help to provide pain relief and ease the symptoms of colds and fevers. It's like natures aspirin. So don't consume willow bark if you're allergic to aspirin.

Wounds becoming infected whilst you're out in the woods can be a serious problem if you aren't going to have access to antibiotics or medical care any time soon. To make an antiseptic wash to help prevent infections in open wounds, simply filter and boil some water to purify it as best as possible and add some pine resin. This will act as a mild antiseptic and help keep infections at bay. You can also gurgle this liquid for tooth and mouth infections. If you're in a rush you can look for wet sap dripping from a tree and apply this directly to the wound.

Another tea you can make is Rosehip tea and is made using, you guessed it, Rosehips. Simply take out the seeds and use only the fleshy red part. This tea is the opposite end of the spectrum from Acorn tea and is useful as a constipation relief. They are also packed with antioxidants and have a very high vitamin content, including vitamin C, meaning they can be used to treat colds and flu.

A great little tip for those of you who have asthma, or if you encounter anyone who has it in a survival situation, is to brew up some nettle tea. Even if you don't have asthma, it's full off all sorts of goodness so it's worth making anyway. It's probably a good idea to hold the nettles over an open fire before putting them in your tea though as this will help to burn away the needles and prevent any nasty stings on the lips.

Another good hack for you is that you can use Birch sap as a sweetener for your tea. Apart from making your tea taste considerably nicer, it will also give you some extra calories and is rich in vitamins and minerals.

7. BUNGEE CORD HACKS

Bungee cords are really useful in a survival situation so they are a great Prepper Hack item.

You can use them to repair broken straps by just replacing it with a bungee cord. They can also be used to attach pouches and other items to Molle webbing. By doing this you will also have bungee cords on you in case you need them. They are also great for securing tents and tarps and holding them in position.

In a bug out situation, you may need to take shelter in an abandoned building for example. Bungee cords can be used to help secure doors that have had the locks previously broken. This also makes them useful for securing entrances in a bug in scenario too, in order to reinforce your doors and help prevent break ins.

Double doors are easy to secure by tying the two handles together. Single doors are a bit harder but if you can hammer a strong nail into the wall you can run a bungee cord from the nail to the door handle. This won't hold forever but it should buy you some extra time and you can easily remove it if you need to make a quick escape, so it may be a better solution that blocking the door off completely.

If you don't have a belt or you break the belt you had with you, then bungee cords make great makeshift belts. You can also use them as suspenders by attaching them to your belt loops.

If you're out in the woods and you need to suspend a lantern, bungee cords work well for this purpose, they can also be used to suspend other things such as suspending a cooking pot over a fire. They could also be used to easily suspend food or supplies to stop animals getting to them or to keep them off the wet ground. The hooked ends of bungee cords make handing things up and taking them down a lot easier than using something like paracord. If you connect a few of them together they also make a good makeshift clothesline.

Another camp application would be, if you are cutting a lot of firewood in advance, you can wrap your logs in a bungee cord and suspend it off of the ground where it may become damp. Then, when you need a log, slip one out of the bundle and the elasticity of the bungee cord will cause it to shrink and keep the rest of the logs held tightly together.

Steve Rayder

8. CHAPSTICK AND VASELINE HACKS

You can put a small amount onto your glasses or goggles and rub it in. Then wipe the lenses off with a cloth to ensure you can see through them properly only leaving a very thin coasting. This will provide you with anti-fog protection.

You can rub Chapstick or Vaseline onto the thread of a flashlight, or anything else with a thread for that matter, and it will help to waterproof it and also lubricate the thread to extend its operational lifespan.

You can apply some Chapstick or Vaseline to the blade of your knife to protect it from water and any potential oxidization and rusting and help to keep it sharp.

It can also be spread onto zippers for some added water resistance. Simply apply a small amount and run the zipper a few times to spread it about. This will also extend the life of zipper and make it much smoother to use.

Chapstick and Vaseline can even be used to plug small pin prick holes in tarps or tents. It may not be the most permanent solution in the world but if it's raining and you need a quick fix this is a good option.

There have been reports and stories of people eating 2 spoons of Vaseline a day to stay alive when they have no food. I wouldn't try it or recommend it but if I was dying of starvation then I would definitely give it a go!

Vaseline can also be used for sealing cuts and grazes to help prevent dirt or contaminants getting in to the wound and potentially causing an infection.

Both Chapstick and Vaseline can be used as an insect repellent. They don't like it as it's greasy so you can put some on your skin to help fend off mosquitos and cover the areas around food or anywhere else you don't want bugs landing.

9. DRINKING STRAW HACKS

The ends of straws can be sealed using fire. The best way to do this is with a multi tool or pliers so that you can crimp down the melted ends for a better waterproof and air tight seal. This means that you can use them for storing various items.

It's best to do this with transparent straws so you can see the contents, or you could use different colours to colour code the contents. If you're using the thicker, larger straws you could even label them with a sharpie.

They can be used in this way to keep matches dry for example. If you can find large straws they can even be used as a waterproof casing for ammo.

You can also make small seasoning packets. This may sound strange but trust me, when you're eating bland food just in order to survive you will appreciate a bit of seasoning on your food more than you realize! This is a good way to store any seasoning or spices you may be able to scavenge in single use, airtight packets. Or you can pre-pack some packets of salt or oil for example.

If you seal them when they are empty and just filled with air they will be buoyant so can be used as a pretty good fishing float.

10. ALUMINUM FOIL HACKS

You can use foil as a makeshift signaling mirror. Obviously a mirror is better as it is more effective at reflecting light but foil will work too. The advantage of using foil for this purpose is that you can use a very large piece making it more obvious to people passing by.

Foil will also make a great light reflector. This can help stop light shining in a direction that you don't want it to which is useful for concealing your location. It also amplifies the effectiveness of your flashlight if you point the beam into a curved or angled reflector by spreading the light and giving it more of a lantern effect. A reflector can also of course be used with a camp fire or a candle in exactly the same way.

If you get a forked stick you can actually wrap tin foil over the forked section and cook on the piece of tin foil by holding or wedging it in place over a fire. It's best to use living, green wood for this task otherwise the stick may catch on fire, break off and drop your food straight into the fire.

You can also simply wrap food in tin foil and place it directly into the embers and use it to make bowls or water containers. This will allow you to boil water to make it sake for drinking. You could even use it as a temporary lid for a bottle or canteen, if you do this while boiling water it will obviously boil much faster.

If you have a flash light or a radio that needs more batteries than you have with you, you can use a ball of tin foil to fill the empty battery space to run it on less batteries.

I have heard that folding up foil and then cutting through it with scissors will sharpen the scissor blades. I'm not 100% convinced on this but it does clean and hone them making them more effective.

It does a good job of cleaning metal objects if you scrub them with crumpled up foil. This is great for using an improvised scouring pad for your mess tins and eating utensils.

Tinder can also be wrapped in tin foil, this is water resistant so will keep your tinder dry but it also means you will have extra tin foil should you need it. As you may have noticed I'm a big fan of all things multi-use so having something that keeps your tinder dry that has all these uses too is great in my opinion.

If you have fishing equipment and no bait, you can wrap a small piece of foil around a hook to make a lure. Most fish will eat fish that are smaller than them and this tin foil could look like a small fish. They will also try eating something if they see it floating through the water to see if it's edible, at which point your hook is in their mouth which is all you need. Predatory fish like perch will be your main target using this method however as what you will have is practically a lure.

11. OTHER HACKS

Paracord Repair Hack

One of the great things about Paracord is that it melts. Usually people only use this to stop the ends of their cord from fraying. However the melted end of a length of Paracord is useful for repairing holes in tarps. Simply set the end of your paracord alight, once it's burning nicely blow it out and quickly apply it to the hole in the tarp. You can hold something flat like a knife on the other side to push it against to help it fill the hole.

Ceramic Mugs

Now obviously mugs can be used to drink out of but there is another surprising use for ceramic mugs. You may have heard of ceramic knife sharpeners, ceramics are great for refining blades. Many ceramic mugs have a rough rim on the bottom, this is the ceramic without the glaze that the rest of the mug has and is great for sharpening your knives.

Bin Liners

Bin liners may seem like a strange survival item, but pack a few of these and you will have an emergency tarp, a makeshift poncho, a backpack cover and a rain water collector! You can even stuff them full of dry leaves for use as a pillow, or put a few of them together for an insulating, water resistant mattress to keep you off of the cold ground.

Makeshift Tent Pegs

If you need to secure a tent or a tarp to the ground in order to secure your shelter, tent pegs can come in very handy. I see people using rocks to weigh things down a lot but tent pegs are a much better solution especially if you need to secure ropes to the ground. However due to weight constraints or even just not thinking you will need them, you may not have any with you. The answer to this problem is incredibly simple yet a lot of people don't think of it. Just take a branch from a tree with a smaller brand protruding from it to use as the hook, and trim it down to the size of a tent peg. You can sharpen the bottom so that it is easier to hammer into the ground. If you don't have a hammer or a mallet, just use a rock.

Sewage

In a breakdown of society services such as electricity, water and gas would go down. One thing that people don't often consider however is the fact that that if the water went off, your toilet wont flush leading to sanitation issues. Well if you have any excess water, from collecting rain water for example, you can just pour a bucket of water into the toilet and gravity will cause it to flush. This means that you can still use your toilet even in a SHTF scenario.

Survival Toothpaste

If you have some Baking Powder or Bicarbonate of Soda, both of these can be used as a toothpaste. If you're out in the woods however, you can use some ground up charcoal as it will act as a mild abrasive that will clean your teeth without damaging them.

Dryer Lint

A great source of free tinder is the lint that collects in your tumble dryer. Keep a bag of this with you and you will have a fantastic source of tinder that will take a spark easily. You can also dramatically increase its burn time by rubbing in some Vaseline or Chapstick. It will also take a spark from a Ferro rod very easily meaning it's nice and easy to light.

Mosquitos

If mosquitos are a problem when you're out in the wilderness there are a few things you can do. A fire will produce smoke that will repel them fairly well, but you can add to its effectiveness by suspending some sage above the fire. For some reason mosquitos hate sage!

Makeshift Snares

Don't overlook guitar strings if you find any on your travels, they make great snares. A lot of guitar strings will already have a loop on the end too making them perfect for this use.

Mouse Traps

Mouse traps are good for catching small animals, the tip here is to make sure you tie them to something and don't just lay them down on the ground and leave them. If an animal is caught by the leg for example, it could easily run off taking your trap with them. So just tie them off to a nearby tree.

Steel Wool

A trick that a lot of people may not know is that you can really easily start a fire using steel wool and a 9 volt battery. Simply take a small handful of steel wool and tap the battery onto it. The fine metal strands will conduct the electricity and burn red hot as the electrical charge dissipates throughout the wool. You can then add some other tinder such as dry grass to catch a flame. This will enable you to start a fire if you have no other form of ignition.

Camp Dry

There are waterproofing sprays available on the market such as Camp Dry that you can simply spray onto items such as your bug out bag to quickly and easily waterproof the fabric. This little trick will help keep your valuable gear dry if you are caught out in the rain.

Chewing Gum Wrapper Fire

This is a great way of starting a fire with nothing but a chewing gum wrapper and a battery. All you have to do it cut the off a strip of chewing gum wrapper that is about 1 inch thick and then cut a V shape out of the middle so that it's very thin in the center. Then press the two ends of the strip onto each end of the battery. The thin section in the middle of the strip will burst into flames within a few seconds. All you need to do from here is have some tinder on standby and use the flame to ignite it.

Ferro Rod Hack

Sometimes you may find it hard to ignite certain tinder with a Ferro rod. A good way to increase the effectiveness of a Ferro rod is to scrape it slowly to create a pile of shavings on your tinder first, then strike it properly over these scrapings. When the spark hits the pile, it will ignite them and they will burn much hotter and be much more effective than just one spark.

Natures Insulation

If you're out in the open and your clothing isn't keeping you warm enough you can stuff dry leaves between your layers of clothing. This will act as an extra layer of insulation against the cold and it really does work well.

Unsafe Safety Matches

Safety matches are designed so that they can only be struck with the striker on the side of the box. You can however still trike them on a pane of glass even if you have lost the box or it's wet for example. You just have to press firmly on the tip with your finger and move it rapidly along the surface of the glass. If you apply a decent amount of pressure then the heat from the friction will be high enough to light it. Just make sure you move your finger away quickly or you could get burned.

Wristwatch Compass

If you're stuck without a compass and but you have a watch or clock, you can use it to find your way using the sun. If you're in the northern hemisphere, point the hour hand at the sun and the point halfway between the hour hand and the 12 will be north. In the southern hemisphere, align the 12 with the sun and the halfway point between the 12 and the hour hand will be north.

Steve Rayder

12. FINAL THOUGHTS

Well I think that about overs it for this installment!

If you want to stay up to date with my regular free book promotions and to also find out about my future releases you can sign up to my mailing list at - www.southshorepublications.com/steverayder

If you would also consider taking the time to leave me an honest review on this book on Amazon I would be extremely appreciative of your feedback.

You can find links to all of my previous books at - http://www.amazon.com/Steve-Rayder/e/B00U0U3Z3E/ or by searching for "Steve Rayder" on Amazon.

Thanks for reading and I hopefully speak to you all in the next book!

Steve Rayder

www.ingramcontent.com/pod-product-compliance
Lightning Source LLC
Chambersburg PA
CBHW070844290526
45795CB00002B/973